# Let's Talk About GOD

## Emmanuel Dixon

# A conversation with a Journal

All scriptures are from KJV and NIV versions of
the Bible unless specified otherwise.
Book and design cover
by Emmanuel Dixon
Photography by Lynda Maupin

# Let's Talk About GOD

When I started writing this book I was only 8, now I'm 9. I thank God for helping me to accomplish it.
I dedicate this book, my First book!

To my mom and my family!

All the time, we should worship God.
Jesus died on the cross for us, so we better
be praising God. If you want to OBEY God,
then never ever quit.
Everyone makes mistakes…
If you're not good at something, just keep
trying. AMEN.

My mom always says "You need to be a
leader and not a follower" Glory to God,
He is a healer.

God can do anything.

*"Do not be ashamed of the gospel".*

*Romans 5:5*

Angels are on their way… Expectation is on
the way. Amen. God is good!!! So good!!!
Amen.
Put on the full armor of God.
God loves everyone the same.

"In this manner, therefore, pray:
Our Father in heaven, Hallowed be
your name. Your kingdom come.
Your will be done on earth as it is
in heaven. Give us this day our
daily bread..."

"The Lord is my strength and my
song, and He has become my
salvation."
He is my God, and I will praise
Him; my father's God, and I will
exalt Him."

Exodus 15:2

Father, we come to you now
in prayer, help us to do what's right,
and not wrong.
Help us to follow the path of
righteousness,
help us to follow your word,
Amen

"He that covered his sins shall not prosper,
but who has confessed and forsake them,
shall have mercy."

God is good so good, I don't even know
how to explain it.

My God is awesome. Amen and Amen.
As far as the east is from the west, so far
that he removed our transgressions for us.

The Lord is my rock.
God wants you to act and think like Christ.

# Prayers Hopes and Dreams Amen.

_____

_____

_____

_____

_____

_____

_____

_____

_____

_____

_____

_____

_____

_____

_____

_____

_____

_____

"And we know that all things work together for good to them that love God, to them who are the called according to His purpose."

Romans 8:28

## Prayers Hopes and Dreams Amen.

_____

_____

_____

_____

_____

_____

_____

_____

_____

_____

_____

_____

_____

_____

_____

_____

_____

One day we were at the movies, my sister handed me the popcorn, and I was trying to grab a lot, so it made the loudest sound. It sounded like a car! But then it sounded like I was playing the drums. I wish I had some drum sticks with me. I want to do that again.

Enjoy your life and never rush to be a grownup. Believe that you can do the stuff that you never could do, and always try new things. Because God gave you talents, and you can't throw them away... If God gave you them, you need to use them. Because God wouldn't give you talents for no reason. You can do anything through Christ that strengthens you.

Why would you want to be a grownup?

_____

_____

_____

_____

What are your talents?

_____

_____

_____

_____

PRAYERS, HOPES AND DREAMS

_____

_____

_____

_____

_____

_____

_____

# What are your favorite colors?

_____

_____

_____

_____

_____

_____

_____

# What foods do you like?

_____

_____

_____

_____

_____

_____

_____

_____

What's your favorite game?

_____

_____

_____

Why do you like it?

_____

_____

_____

_____

_____

_____

_____

_____

_____

"For God so loved the world that He gave His only begotten son and whosoever believeth in Him shall not perish but have eternal life." John 3:16 Amen and Amen!

God is Alpha and Omega Beginning and the End.

When did you except Christ as your Savior?

_____

_____

_____

_____

_____

_____

_____

_____

_____

_____

_____

_____

_____

_____

_____

_____

Please God help us to follow your commandment's this is my favorite…

"Thou shall have no other gods before me."

Exodus 20:3

What did you learn?

_____

_____

_____

How did it inspire you?

_____

_____

_____

Why do you love God?

_____

_____

_____

God created... fish, bees, sharks, octopuses, tigers, and birds. I could name one million things that He made, but that would take up to much of the book!

Obey your parents in the Lord because
it could be
life saving tips

Obey your parents because...

_____

_____

_____

_____

Do you love God?

_____

_____

_____

_____

My mom inspired me so much!!!!!!!!!!

How does your mom inspire you?

_____

_____

_____

_____

# Believe in yourself!

You can do it
Prayers, hopes and dreams

_____

_____

_____

_____

_____

_____

_____

_____

_____

_____

_____

_____

_____

_____

_____

_____

"…But Noah found grace in the eyes of the Lord…"

Genesis 6:8

"Trust in the LORD with all your heart and lean not on your own understanding; in all your ways submit to him, and he will make your paths straight."

Proverbs 3:5-6

# Prayers

_____

_____

_____

_____

_____

_____

_____

_____

_____

_____

_____

_____

_____

_____

_____

_____

# Love God with all your heart.

## Notes

_____

_____

_____

_____

_____

_____

Love your parents.


Love your neighbors.

What books do you like to read?

_____

_____

_____

_____

_____

## What do you like about yourself?

_____

_____

_____

_____

## What do you think about life?

_____

_____

_____

## Notes

_____

_____

_____

_____

_____

_____

_____

_____

# Prayers hopes and dreams

_____

_____

_____

_____

_____

_____

_____

_____

_____

_____

_____

_____

_____

_____

_____

_____

_____

"And the Lord said unto Moses,
Lo, I come unto thee in a thick
cloud, that the people may hear
when I speak with thee, and
believe thee forever."

Exodus 19:9

# How do know you love God?

_____

_____

_____

_____

_____

_____

## Notes

_____

_____

_____

_____

_____

_____

_____

_____

Prayers hopes and dreams

_____

_____

_____

_____

_____

_____

_____

What are all the things you like to do?

_____

_____

_____

_____

_____

_____

_____

We love him, because he
first loved us.
1 John 4:19

# Why does God love you?

_____

_____

_____

_____

_____

_____

_____

_____

_____

_____

_____

_____

_____

_____

_____

## Notes

_____

_____

_____

_____

**God loves and He always will.**

Why do you love your parents?

_____

_____

_____

_____

_____

_____

_____

One day it was my mom's birthday, and my sister and I planned the whole thing. We did so much for her. We opened doors for her and everything! She said that she loved it! Always treat your mom with respect amen! God loves it when we are being nice to each other, but He hates it if you're acting like a bully.

What do you like about the world?

_____

_____

_____

Do you pray once a day? Or more?

_____

_____

_____

Do you obey your parents?

_____

_____

_____

"It is God that girded me with strength, and maketh my way perfect. He maketh my feet like hinds' feet and setteth me upon high places. He teacheth my hands to war, so that a bow of steel is broken by mine arms. Thou hast given me a shield of salvation: and thy right hand hath holden me up, and thy gentleness hath made me great. Thou hast enlarged my steps under me, that my feet did not slip..."

Psalms 18:32-36

One day we were running the Bluegrass 10,000. It was our first time, and we started late... but my mom said, "It's not how you start, but *that* you **FINISH!**" Never ever give up! Keep on keeping on no matter what happens. Keep the faith HALLELUYAH

Thank you God for helping every one of us to keep pushing on, and to trust in God. Amen thank you for being God and blessing us with your strength, and especially courage. We basically use courage all the time. We use it to preach to people and help people. Hallelujah

"...Be strong and of good courage; be not afraid, neither be thou dismayed: for the Lord thy God is with thee whithersoever thou goest."

Joshua 1:9

"The Lord is my rock, and my fortress, and my deliverer; My God, My strength, in whom I will trust; my buckler, and the horn of my salvation, and my high tower."

Psalm 18:2

One day I was climbing a tree with my sister, and then I saw a big ant getting ready to crawl on me…
so I jumped off! I said that to say, don't be afraid of stuff. God is with you. God is everywhere.

God creates masterpieces and put that creative ability in all of us. I like to paint. I do it a lot, but the real painter is God. HALLELUYAH! God painted the whole world. He painted the sky, the ground, you name it… God did it. So we could never paint as well as G-O-D.

Thank God for the ability to make things, draw, and paint well, but, if you win a drawing contest remember God got in first place.

God is amazing super awesome I'll praise God for the rest of my life.
You can do it no matter what, keep pushing, and trust in God. Keep faith… God is with you…just take can't out of you vocabulary. Hallelujah! You can do it! You can do it! Trust in God and listen to Him.


God bless you and may God give you everlasting love.

Some Important things to Remember:

Divided we fall, together we stand. Amen.

My God is almighty powerful.

Treat others as you want them to treat you.

**You can overcome obstacles.
You just have to have faith, trust, and
don't listen to *naysayers* because they
don't know who their messing with!**

**God is in Control!**

# God Loves You!

This book, I believe will help you to have a closer relationship with God.
This book is amazing and is for all ages.
I want to thank my mom that also made a book, and my sister that made a book too.

So let's talk about God Amen

**Continually...**

*9 7 8 0 6 9 2 3 0 0 5 7 2 *